Elusive Truth

Four Photographers at Manzanar

Elusive Truth

Four Photographers at Manzanar

by

Gerald H. Robinson

Introduction by Archie Miyatake

Carl Mautz Publishing

Nevada City, California

2002

First Edition
Copyright 2002 Carl Mautz Publishing

ISBN 1-887694-23-4 (Cloth) 500 copies
ISBN 1-887694-24-2 (Paper) 1000 copies

Cataloging-in-publication data
Elusive truth: four photographers at Manzanar (Ansel Adams, Clem Albers, Dorothea Lange, Toyo Miyatake)/Gerald H. Robinson
p. cm.
Includes bibliographical references and index
ISBN: 1-887694-23-4 cloth
    1-887694-24-2 paper
1. Manzanar War Relocation Center-Pictorial works. 2. Japanese Americans-Evacuation and relocation, 1942-1945-Pictorial works.
I. Robinson, Gerald H. II. Title
D769.8.A6 A63 2002

Front cover: Entrance to Manzanar by Ansel Adams
Back cover: *Ireito* (memorial tower) built by Manzanar internees, calligraphy by Rev.
    Shinji Nagatomi, photographed by Toyo Miyatake
Frontispiece: Camera constructed surreptitiously at Manzanar by Toyo Miyatake

Photographs by Ansel Adams are courtesy of the Library of Congress

Photographs by Clem Albers and Dorothea Lange are courtesy of the National Archives

Photographs by Toyo Miyatake are courtesy of Archie Miyatake and the Miyatake Family

Carl Mautz Publishing
229 Commercial St PMB 522
Nevada City CA 95959
530-478-1610 Fax 530-478-0772
www.carlmautz.com

To Mutsumi Inoue Robinson,
with thanks for her love and encouragement

CONTENTS

Cutting the Barbed Wire by Toyo Miyatake

PREFACE

Retirement from the practice of law has given me an opportunity to renew my interest in the history of photography and to confront a gnawing memory of my high school locker-mate leaving to go to "camp" because he was half Japanese and half Korean. Over the years I followed the legal struggles of the *Nikkei* to vindicate themselves and gain some measure of indemnity for the humiliating wrong the United States perpetrated upon them during World War II.

This book resulted from a hard look at the photographs made at Manzanar Relocation Camp, one of the eleven such places in which about 110,000 Americans of Japanese descent were incarcerated solely because of their race. The study of the pictures, made by four accomplished photographers all seeking to reveal the truth, demonstrates that the "truth" of photodocumentarians is both fragile and elusive: a kind of still version of the Japanese film *Rashomon* that told of the same event seen through different eyes. At variance from *Rashomon*, however, the four photographers chronicled Manzanar at different times, under various restrictions, and when its internees were under evolving living conditions and circumstances. The underlying truth about the "relocation" of the American Japanese was concealed from the photographers (along with everyone else) by the U.S. Government, and what was visible to the photographers was shifting, fragmentary, and elusive.

Although many have helped in my endeavor, I have full responsibility for what follows. In particular, I want to thank the great historian of photography Dr. Peter H. Bunnell, a friend for many years, who cast a frank and not altogether approving eye on early drafts; Tom Robinson, an astute and perceptive writer; my wife Mutsumi, for her patience and her help in translating documents from Japanese into English; Archie Miyatake, for his insights into his father Toyo's work; Joe Rosenthal, for his memories about his friend and colleague Clem Albers; and to Carl Mautz, who was ready to risk both time and money to make the book a reality.

Gerald Robinson, June, 2002

Norito Takamoto, Bruce Sansui, and Masaaki Imamura by Toyo Miyatake

INTRODUCTION

My father was Toyo Miyatake, one of the photographers whose work is featured in this book. He was born in Japan, but he completely accepted the American way of life. He was comfortable being with his Caucasian friends and communicating with them. He could have lived a comfortable life in Japan, but he preferred to make his home in Los Angeles where he operated a successful photography studio.

With the outbreak of World War II and the enactment of Executive Order 9066, everybody of Japanese descent, including American citizens, were ordered to evacuate the West Coast. Most of them were placed in internment camps. Manzanar, an abandoned town a few miles outside of Lone Pine, high in the Eastern Sierra Nevada Mountains, was such an internment camp. It was there that Toyo Miyatake and his family, including myself, were sent. Anything Government agents considered contraband was confiscated, including cameras, which were the tools of my father's trade.

Toyo's life was devoted to photography. For Toyo, life without his camera was a big blow. In spite of the turmoil caused by our forced relocation, he wanted to record life during the internment years. Conditions in the windy, dusty high desert at Manzanar were very difficult. After three or four months of camp life, my father spoke to me privately. He said, "As a photographer, I have a responsibility to record the camp life so this kind of thing will never happen again." He then showed me a lens and shutter and some film holders he had smuggled into camp. "I am going to find a carpenter and have a box made so I can record the camp life," he said. Within a short time, he did this, and because of his foresight, he was able to carry out this work. His photographs taken during the incarceration show not only the hardship, but also how Japanese Americans made the best of the situation.

My father's legacy, and the suffering of 110,000 other Americans of Japanese descent, should stand as a lesson to America to avoid extreme measures, even when fear abounds. What happened to Japanese-Americans was not the first, and unfortunately, not the last, occasion of harsh oppression of "foreigners" among us, people of different races, religions, or culture whom we fear during times of crisis. Today America is again under attack. Toyo Miyatake would defend our nation, but also seek to preserve the human and legal rights of every person.

Archie Miyatake, June, 2002

The Camp in the High Desert by Ansel Adams

THE CAMP AT MANZANAR

After the sudden attack on the United States at Pearl Harbor on December 7, 1941, the American government moved swiftly against its 120,000 citizens and residents of Japanese ancestry. On February 19, 1942, President Franklin D. Roosevelt signed Executive Order 9066. It authorized a curfew and evacuation of any groups designated by the military commanders in their complete discretion; it created not martial law in the Western United States, but rather, arbitrary military rule. Pursuant to this Order, all persons of Japanese ancestry were placed under tight curfew and eventually evacuated to relocation centers. Even though 80% of them were native-born U.S. citizens, all of them were assumed to be security risks. In short order, they were registered, removed from their homes and livelihoods, and placed in eleven concentration camps euphemistically called "relocation centers." These establishments were usually placed on surplus federal land and were scattered from Idaho to the swamps of Arkansas. They were operated by the War Relocation Authority (WRA), a federal New Deal-like agency manned largely by self-proclaimed liberals, and specially created to fulfill its custodial function.[1]

One of the largest relocation camps was located at Manzanar, California, in Owens Valley, east of the Sierra Nevada. It was surrounded, like all the WRA camps, by barbed wire and machine guns in guard towers manned by a detachment of U.S. Army Military Police. It officially opened in March 1942, first as an Army assembly center, and later, as a WRA Relocation camp. It was administered by a Project Director and 82 other Caucasian WRA employees broken into sections including Reports, Legal, Community Services, Welfare, Health, Education, Community Enterprises, Internal Security (intra-camp police), Agriculture, Fire Control, Manufacturing, Public Works, Transportation and Supply, Employment and Housing, and Administration—a veritable bureaucratic ghetto operated by Caucasians.

The fenced camp occupied about 400 acres of a 6000-acre military reservation. Its buildings were essentially tar-papered military barracks grouped into blocks with firebreaks between them. Each block had a mess hall and a washing, toilet and shower facility. Offices, schools and the hospital were all located in barracks; camp managers lived in relative comfort beyond the barbed wire.

Owens Valley had once been a lush farmland—"Manzanar" is Spanish for "apple orchard." But the water in the valley had nearly all been drained away to nourish burgeoning Los Angeles, leaving behind a desert.[2] Freezing in winter and blistering hot in the dusty dry summers, Manzanar faced west toward the majestic Sierra Nevada, the "Range of Light," and east toward the lower but still impressive Inyo Range.

Into this environment about 11,000 ethnic Japanese, of all ages, American citizens and noncitizens, laborers and professionals, rich, poor, and middle class, were conveyed by armed military forces to the uncompleted "assembly center"[3] and eventually delivered into the hands of the WRA. None of the internees, as they were called, had been convicted of a crime, nor had any been found to be disloyal or a security threat to the United States.

However, Manzanar's population soon began to decline as efforts were made to "relocate" American Japanese, at first away from the West Coast, but after the Supreme Court's 1944 Endo decision, anywhere.[4] The camp officially closed November 25, 1945.

Four photographers, Ansel Adams, Clem Albers, Dorothea Lange, and Toyo Miyatake, worked at Manzanar, photographing the American Japanese who were interned there. Each photographer, except Miyatake who was an internee during most of its existence, saw the camp when it was in a different condition physically, socially and politically. Each brought exceptional professional and varied experience to the task. Moreover, with the exception of Miyatake, there is no evidence that they had any profound insights about the evacuees, their history, or their rapidly changing culture. In that way, they reflected the segregated America of the mid-twentieth century.

In fact, the attitudes and values of the rapidly diminishing *Issei* (first generation, born in Japan) were strikingly different from those of their U.S. born children, the *Nisei*, and of their grandchildren, the *Sansei*. As with most immigrant groups in the

United States, acculturation swiftly undermined old values and ways and imprinted on younger generations uniquely American traits: fluency in English, Western religions, and independence in thought and action. Moreover, the American Japanese were in large measure isolated from Caucasian society, living as they did in "Japan towns" in a few West Coast cities, or scattered in rural areas.

Only the efforts of the evacuees themselves made Manzanar livable. Often they used scrap wood, cloth and other scrounged materials to weatherproof the barracks, build partitions between families, and simulate something of a home-like atmosphere. Vegetable gardens were started to supplement Army rations. Eventually school systems, hospitals and newspapers were created, mostly employing the American Japanese professionals augmented by WRA employees: necessary services like shoe repair, beauty and barber shops, clothing manufacture and cleaning, and small cooperative stores, began to operate. Over time evacuees developed adult classes in a variety of artistic and cultural activities, and produced a substantial and impressive body of art and handicraft.[5]

As the internees set about to create an environment for an indefinite future, they were employed not only to build their own prison but also in developing and farming adjacent fields and, at Manzanar, in a factory to make camouflage netting. They were paid far below the minimum wage at the time.[6] Largely through their own efforts and ingenuity, Manzanar's inmates shaped a small but functioning town that more than paid its way financially. Ironically, almost as soon as the WRA assumed control of the relocation program, it devised procedures whereby evacuees who were certified to be loyal could leave the camps to go to interior parts of the United States.[7] Later, emptying the centers was promoted vigorously by a system of travel grants and loans for residents with relocation plans approved by the WRA.[8]

The American Japanese community (known collectively as *Nikkei* in Japanese) has been inaccurately characterized as passively submitting to internment. In truth, there were many opinions among the *Nikkei* as to how they should react. Some urged compliance with the military orders. A small percentage of *Issei* sympathized with

Japan and asked to be repatriated in the exchanges of civilians that took place during the hostilities. In between were the vast majority who absorbed the shock of the internment and tried to make the best of it, and who, from time to time and in increasing numbers, left the camps to go to places within the interior of the U.S., or joined the Army.

Overt protest took several forms. Some American Japanese disobeyed the exclusion and curfew orders and were prosecuted and convicted when their constitutional arguments lost in the Supreme Court. Others demanded self-government in the camps, with varying success. A few protests in the camps led to riots, some deaths, and ultimately the segregation at Tule Lake, California, of those whom the WRA dubbed "troublemakers." Several hundred *Nisei* refused to be drafted into the segregated Army and went to prison.

To the shame of the courts, none of the test cases were successful, at least until 1945 when the Supreme Court decided <u>In re Endo</u>. But the legal challenges illuminate the strong feelings of a large segment of the affected population. Forty years after the event, in 1982, the Commission on Wartime Relocation and Internment of Civilians (CWRIC) exposed the contrived and false basis for the evacuation program; it found that there was no military necessity for the relocation. This conclusion was validated by subsequently discovered documents and the judgments of courts that set aside the wartime convictions of protesters.[9]

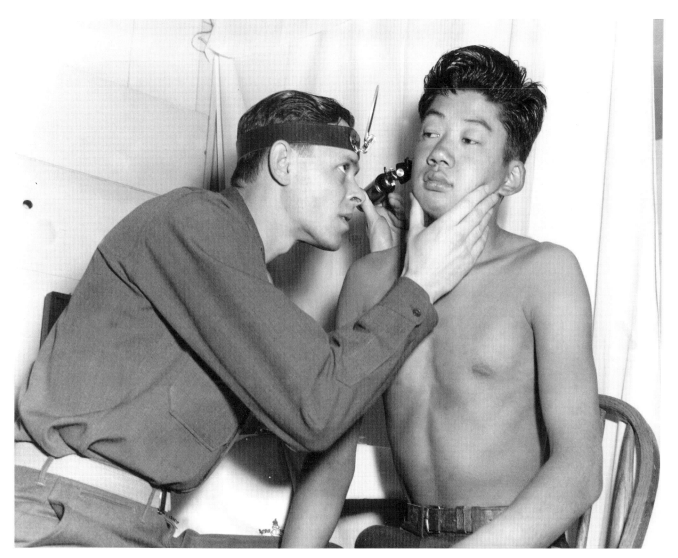

Leo Uchida being examined for induction into the U.S. Army by Toyo Miyatake

Mount Williamson and Barracks by Toyo Miyatake

THE PROJECTS

In order to determine whether the four photographers successfully portrayed Manzanar, one must consider not only the physical state of the camp, even as it changed over time, but also the attitudes, feelings, and social relationships of the American Japanese. It may be impossible for one not directly affected to fully absorb the trauma and the lasting effects of incarceration, loss of property, and even more important, injury to self esteem and family relationships that resulted from the evacuation and internment.

Moreover, to be sure, documentary photography has built-in limitations: by definition, photographs deal with surfaces and, some would say, superficial facts. Obvious expressions in the faces, postures, clothing and demeanor of subjects can be captured in still photographs, but what feelings, attitudes, values, hopes, and aspirations, for example, may be buried beneath the reach of optics and beyond the ability of film to register? In simple and clear-cut situations, photographic documents can approximate the whole story, but even in the compelling wartime images of a master such as Robert Capa, for example, the secret fears, revulsions, and hatreds of those upon whom he focused can only be guessed.

Yet the task of the Manzanar photographers was to display more than the barracks and surrounding scenery, more than the physical inadequacies of camp life, important as they might have been. They needed to cut beneath the outward appearances of people caught up in events solely because of their race, and portray in the profound sense of that term, and as far as possible, their fears and concerns, their feelings of betrayal and mistrust, their loss of pride and dignity, and possibly, their hopes and aspirations.

The Manzanar photographers did not perform in a vacuum or even break dramatic new ground. In Europe, photographers like John Thompson, James Annan, and August Sander had recorded social realities in their distinctive ways. The documentary tradition in American photography had, even in 1942, a long and distinguished pedigree that included luminaries such as the Civil War photographers Matthew Brady and Timothy H. O'Sullivan, and recorders of civilian society, among them Lewis Hine, Jacob Riis, Edward Curtis, and Adam Clark Vroman.

In fact, the Manzanar photographers, and others who documented both World War II and the internment of American Japanese, in a sense took up and carried forward the photography of Roy E. Stryker's Farm Security Administration (FSA) photography project, as well as the New York Photo League's efforts to systematically teach social documentation with the camera.

But even before America's official involvement in World War II, the FSA (along with many other New Deal social and economic programs) was being dissolved and it was fated to disappear into the wartime mobilization. Some of the FSA photographers were hired by the WRA, notably Russell Lee and Dorothea Lange, as part of the Photographic Division that was headquartered in its Denver field office.[10] The Division's task was to make a visual record of the evacuation of the Japanese and the operation of some, if not all, of the camps. It is interesting to speculate why the WRA wanted photographs of its operations; it used only a few images in occasional reports to illustrate its benevolence, and the Army selected some for its final report on the internment program. The rest of the pictures were placed in the National Archives, from which various writers have selected illustrations from time to time.

Of the four photographers whose work we consider, only Lange and Albers were on the WRA payroll. Adams was a volunteer and Miyatake was interned with his family. Clearly, the four photographers' backgrounds, photographic techniques and the timing of their Manzanar projects, as well as their political and social attitudes, can explain to some degree the distinctive images each produced.

All of the photographers who worked at Manzanar were manipulated covertly and overtly by the government, even to the point of having some photographs suppressed by the military and the WRA.[11] Photographers were told what they could and could not photograph, and military police sometimes accompanied them as they worked, steering them away from subjects deemed objectionable by the authorities.[12]

It must have been a fine line to walk for a photographer to record the camps without making apparent the wretched conditions under which the evacuees lived, how much they must have resented their confinement, and that for many of them during most of the war, there was no way for them to leave.[13]

Tom Koybayashi by Ansel Adams

FOUR PHOTOGRAPHERS

ANSEL ADAMS

When the United States became involved in the war in 1941, Ansel Adams was over-age for the draft,[14] but he wanted desperately to assist in the war effort. He had already established himself as a protégé of Alfred Stieglitz and a rising fine art photographer with important exhibitions behind him. He believed that the German and Japanese militarists were evil and needed to be destroyed. He was as passionately patriotic as he was a committed environmentalist.

Meanwhile, Edward Steichen was commissioned by the Navy to establish a corps of documentary photographers to record its battles. Adams wanted to join, but Steichen offered him a job running a darkroom, a proposal Adams rejected as insulting.[15]

In 1942, Adams joined the faculty of the Art Center School in Los Angeles expecting to train military photographers. Instead, he was asked to teach basic dark-room processes to defense industry workers and soldiers, and methods of photographing corpses to civil defense staff.

Dismayed, Adams went back to his base in Yosemite in 1943. Soon, an old Sierra Club friend, Ralph Merritt, arrived. He had just been appointed director of the Manzanar War Relocation Camp about 150 miles away. He invited Adams to document its internees and Adams eagerly accepted. [16] He was motivated not only by his desire to help the war effort, but also by his perception of injustice in the exclusion orders against the American Japanese.

A personal experience heightened his concern. Within a few days after the Pearl Harbor attack, his elderly American Japanese gardener and a longtime family retainer, Harry Oye, was detained as an enemy alien and held in a government hospital in Missouri. Although loyal to the United States, Oye was an *Issei* and thus ineligible for U.S. citizenship. Despite ill health, he was taken into custody because he was a leader in the Japanese community. Although Adams admitted that Oye had been well-treated, he was nevertheless outraged that Oye was arrested at all.

Adams made several trips to Manzanar in the fall and winter of 1943 and the spring of 1944. He used his own film and supplies and, unlike Lange and Albers, was not on the government payroll. Because the eastbound exit from Yosemite over the Tioga Pass road was closed in the winters, Adams had to make some trips to Manzanar via a long detour through Bakersfield and then north up the east side of the Sierras. But he also made side trips and stops on his way to and from Manzanar to photograph the stunning scenery. Some of his strongest landscape works, such as "Mount Williamson," "Mount Whitney," and "Winter Sunrise, The Sierra Nevada from Lone Pine," were done during this period.

Adams had two themes he sought to express through his Manzanar pictures. He wrote: "The object of the pictures is to clarify the distinction of the loyal citizens of Japanese ancestry, and the disloyal Japanese citizens and aliens (I might say Japanese-loyal aliens) who are stationed mostly in internment camps."[17]

In a diary, he emphasized the importance of the distinction being made by the WRA: it was "doing a magnificent job, and is firm and ruthless in its definitions of true loyalty."[18]

The other theme was Adams' admiration for the American Japanese in overcoming an injustice and building a livable community, a process that he believed accelerated their passage into full American citizenship. He wished to depict this transition visually and use the photographs to convince the American public of the qualities and values of American Japanese.

A group of Adams' Manzanar photographs and his accompanying text was published in *Born Free and Equal*.[19] A show based on the prints and text was assembled and hung at Manzanar for viewing by the residents in January 1944, and it was then shown at the Museum of Modern Art in New York. To emphasize Adams' sense that the evacuation was a great injustice, he included in *Born Free and Equal* quotations from Secretary of the Interior Harold Ickes (who was strongly opposed to the exclusion and relocation program) and Abraham Lincoln, and the Fourteenth Amendment to the U.S. Constitution.

Apparently Adams submitted the book for review by the authorities, because he mentions that the photographs and the facts in the text were checked and approved by the Manzanar Project Director (Ralph Merritt). Ultimately, before he died in 1984, Adams donated his Manzanar work to the Library of Congress.[20]

In 1989, a larger selection of Adams' prints was included in *Manzanar*[21] along with a commentary by John Hersey.

Adams' Manzanar work is unique among the work of the four photographers in that he published a selection of the prints and showed them in a prestigious New York art museum. Thus, they were intended for a wider audience than that which Lange, Albers, and Miyatake probably had in mind. Despite her strong negative feelings toward the injustice done the American Japanese, Lange was employed by the WRA and surely knew that her work would not only belong to the Government but also be subject to its control. There is no record of Albers' intentions about his relocation pictures. So also with Toyo Miyatake; although not directly employed by the WRA, he photographed at its sufferance. He was ultimately permitted to work rather freely at Manzanar as well as to conduct a small portrait studio, but his ability to replenish his photographic supplies and bring in his equipment was directly authorized and controlled by the Project Director. Like Lange and Albers, Miyatake apparently did not write about his pictures or his reactions to his incarceration and that of his family.

Adams' Manzanar photographs are clearly recognizable as "Adams;" they are executed with great technical skill and careful attention to lighting and expression. Compositions are strong and flexible, but controlled. The large scale landscapes were made with an 8x10 view camera; medium range pictures were done with a 5x7 Zeiss Juwel folding camera, and for portraits he used a 4x5 Graflex reflex camera.[22] Each piece of equipment was carefully chosen as the best available tool for the job intended.

Given Adams' intention to show the public the loyalty, courage, resourcefulness and determination of most of the American Japanese evacuees in both a book and a show, his choice of equipment was admirable. Both the large and medium film formats enabled him to make prints of exhibition quality and with the detail and tonal gradations necessary for a first-rate presentation.[23]

Adams came to Manzanar well over a year after it had become a Relocation Center and after the deadly riot there in December 1942. By that time, its inhabitants had established farming, industries, shops, limited self-government, schools, and the *Manzanar Free Press*. Started with over 11,000 evacuees, the camp's population had dwindled by half when Adams first arrived. Many internees had been granted "indefinite leave" to go to locations away from either coast, and a few young men enlisted in the Army. Two of Adams' pictures show people departing from Manzanar.

If Adams felt that the experience of being uprooted and incarcerated was unjust, he also believed that it might become a path to growth and even renewal for the American Japanese, propelling them toward greater achievements and acceptance as citizens of the United States. Even the bleak but imposing landscape surrounding Manzanar, he thought, had a beneficial effect on their souls by providing spiritual sustenance. "I have been accused of sentimental conjecture when I suggest that the beauty of the natural scene stimulated the people in the camp…and many of the people spoke to me of these qualities and their thankfulness for them."[24]

In his portraits, Adams focused on his subjects as individuals who also happened to be American Japanese. His heads for the most part are dignified and even heroic.[25] A few people seem casual; most seem reserved and formal. Some smile, but many do not. One who doesn't is Harry Sumida, shown in the camp hospital. Mr. Sumida was a wounded U.S. Navy veteran of the Spanish-American War of 1898; he was taken out of a Veterans Administration Hospital and removed to Manzanar!

In Adams' pictures taken at long range, the great Sierras often hover over the camp and emphasize its isolation, suggesting barriers even more formidable than the barbed wire and machine gun towers around its perimeter. The peaks are always registered with clarity, in contrast with Miyatake's mountain backgrounds that are less distinct and thus rather menacing. Adams' images of people picking crops make them appear almost insignificant in the grand landscape. Sometimes, a high camera angle betrays the existence of elevated guard towers that were not permitted to be photographed. In both distance and medium range scenes, Adams depicts the rows of drab and gloomy barracks marching across the flat valley floor, a depressing sight indeed, contradicting the message of "normalcy."

Most of the middle range images also show the shabby background of tarpaper covered barracks; interiors depicted seem almost normal, until one looks carefully and sees the dangling light fixtures, crude walls, and home-made furniture, as well as the overwhelming feeling of temporariness. Cozy though some may seem to the casual viewer, these crowded spaces lack the element of personal choice that most people—but not the internees—have: "We choose to make our home look this way!"

One picture taken at the camp entrance shows a benign and handsome rustic sign—"Manzanar War Relocation Center"—like one might see upon entering a National Park. The picture also includes, however, the guard post with its small but legible "Military Police" sign, revealing the true purpose of the camp: to hold people against their will.

Adams used only a few group pictures in his book: collections of students, a family here, a choir practicing there. Some subjects smile politely at him; the choir seems devoid of the joy of making music.[26]

Karin B. Ohrn has compared Adams' and Lange's work at Manzanar. She contends that to Lange, the importance of a documentary work was its social significance but that to Adams it was "the virtuosity of its aesthetic performance."[27] But while Adams was always a concerned craftsman, his objectives were never so limited. His means were chosen to accomplish well-defined ends, always emotionally expressive. In the case of Manzanar, it is just that Adams' documentary purposes were quite different than those of Lange.

Obviously neither Lange nor Adams knew that they were victims of government deception. Lange, who had fought her own battles with the bureaucrats, may have had suspicions, but if she did, there is no verbal record of them and none show in her work. Adams believed with his friend and climbing colleague Director Ralph Merritt that the relocation was a wartime necessity, a prudent move by a concerned government.[28] Now we know differently, but during World War II, virtually everyone supported the American war effort after Pearl Harbor; few questioned the measures the government claimed were needed to attain victory.

Adams believed that the American Japanese had managed to rise above the injustice imposed upon them and to build a functioning community at Manzanar. This deeply impressed him. But he was not there to witness the initial traumatic influx of people into the unfinished camp, as were Albers and Lange, nor did he suffer the daily oppression felt by internees like Miyatake. The riot that claimed two lives was past,[29] and "troublemakers" had been removed to the penal camp at Tule Lake, California. People were leaving Manzanar and within a year the Supreme Court announced in Endo[30] that no loyal U.S. citizen could be detained in the camps against his or her will. In other words, Adams was photographing Manzanar at what might be considered its apogee: a developed community whose members had begun to hope for, and to expect, freedom.

Even so, he was disturbed by the anomaly of *Nisei* soldiers on leave visiting their families still held in the camp, and he conjectured how difficult it must have been for them and their incarcerated relatives. It was, Adams said, "a severe contradiction of the principles for which they were fighting the war…. It was a nightmare situation."[31]

Regardless of Adams' perception of the hypocrisy and injustice of the expulsion and incarceration of loyal Americans because of their race, there is more than a hint that he viewed the relocation as a positive act of social engineering. After the "disloyal elements"[32] had been sorted out, he felt that scattering the American Japanese around the United States was "far better for them than re-concentration in racial districts or groups. They wish to prove their worth as individuals…."[33] Such a patronizing viewpoint is startling now, but in the context of the New Deal and its popular ideology, it is understandable.[34] It does reemphasize, however, how much Adams focused on his subjects as admirable people whom he believed had overcome adversity.

Indeed, Adams believed that his photographic message of hope and the supremacy of the spirit of a people who were unjustly treated was of the utmost significance. In an interview in 1974, Adams said, referring to his Manzanar pictures: "So I really think I can go on record as saying that from a social point of view that's the most important thing I've done or can do, as far as I know."[35]

"Pioneers" consult with Caucasian supervisor by Clem Albers

CLEM ALBERS

Clem Albers was born around 1903 in Michigan. He grew up in Berkeley, California, and as a teenager, became a photographer for the San Francisco *Bulletin* and later, the *Chronicle*. He was either employed by, or loaned to, the WRA early in its operations.

Albers photographed the assembly of Japanese Americans as they boarded buses and trains and as they disembarked at their destinations. He worked at Manzanar for a couple of days in early April 1942 when the camp was still under construction and military police units there were living in army tents. The National Archives include 381 WRA photographs by Albers, of which 107 were made at Manzanar.

The low overall count[36] suggests that Albers' tenure with the WRA was short. The photographs were also spread between Manzanar, Poston, Tule Lake, and the evacuation and assembly process. Apparently he left the WRA to became a Warrant Officer photographer in the Maritime Service for the rest of World War II. He then returned to the *Chronicle,* became its Chief Photographer, and died in San Francisco in October 1991. He was a close friend of the Pulitzer Prize-winning photographer Joe Rosenthal, who provided information and valuable insights about him for this book.

Unfortunately, only a few of Albers' Manzanar photographs have been published, but all of them can be viewed on the National Archives website (http://www.archives.gov) as well as that of the University of California at Berkeley (http://www.oac.cdblib.org/dynaweb/ead/calher/jvac/). Some were included in *Executive Order 9066*.[37]

Albers' experience as a press photographer made him skeptical about politicians and official pronouncements and, although not vocal about it, he viewed the mass evacuation of American Japanese with distaste—a disdain that is smuggled into the two-edged images. For example, he showed aged American Japanese men and women and tiny children being helped by soldiers from evacuation trains; this may display military compassion to some, but others may ask why they were there in the first place. American Japanese so-called "volunteer pioneers" work at Manzanar to construct their own concentration camp, but they do so under armed guard.

Albers did not hesitate to reveal the primitive conditions into which the evacuees were placed, and their grim and frightened expressions. A particularly poignant image, for example, shows a window of a train arriving at Lone Pine, California, on the journey to Manzanar. Inside, peering through the dirty glass, is a small child somber with fear.

In other photographs, Albers shows the incoming evacuees lining up for injections, nailing up signs, building their barracks, and trying to clear sagebrush. In some, the military police are at assembly, armed with rifles. A woman gets a pail of water from a hydrant; there is no running water in the barracks. An elderly man is examined by an evacuee physician in the newly established hospital; the WRA has neutralized this "grave threat" to national security. One particularly telling image shows evacuee children penned in a truck, looking through the slats that serve as bars, identity tags hanging from their clothing.

Finally, there is a young woman looking out a doorway from a dark room, watching another girl walking by in Japanese "geta," the tall wooden shoes that Albers' caption mentions as being particularly useful in dust—plentiful at Manzanar.

Albers established the facts in a professional and incisive way. His pictures speak clearly for those who care to look, and the message is one of sharp irony.

"Pioneers" building the camp by Clem Albers

Joe Blamey (born in Japan) by Dorothea Lange

DOROTHEA LANGE

In 1941, when she joined the WRA staff, Dorothea Lange had already established her reputation as a documentary photographer. She was born in 1895 and died in 1965. Like Alfred Stieglitz, Lange was born into a German immigrant family in Hoboken, New Jersey. She grew up in the tenements of New York City while her mother worked in garment sweatshops; from an early age she observed the varied cultures of New York and developed an understanding of its social problems and empathy for its victims. Perhaps this process was enhanced by her polio-crippled leg. "Cripples," she said, "know about each other."

Lange became a portrait photographer, attended Clarence H. White's photography classes, and in 1913 or 1914, she was hired by Arnold Genthe. In 1919, she moved to San Francisco where she later met photographers such as Imogen Cunningham and Ansel Adams. During the economic depression Lange became interested in photographing the unemployed, the downcast and the impoverished. She gradually made the transition from the studio to the street.[38]

By the middle 1930s Lange had closed her studio and was fully engaged in documentary photography, selling her work to a range of magazines. About that time, she met Dr. Paul Taylor, an associate professor of economics at the University of California, Berkeley. Both Taylor and Lange eventually obtained divorces and married each other. Taylor was well versed in the effects of economic depression at the human level, and clearly brought another dimension of understanding to Lange. Leveraging Taylor's insights, Lange developed a philosophy: to make documentary photographs to effect social change.

In August 1935, Roy E. Stryker hired her to work for the Historical Section of the Resettlement Administration, which later became the Farm Security Administration.

It is important to understand the methods Stryker used in the FSA photography project. He had been trained as an economist and was a close associate at Columbia University of Rexford Guy Tugwell, one of President Franklin D. Roosevelt's early collection of advisors called the "Brain Trust." Tugwell was the architect of some of the New Deal programs that were to change America's economy and way of life forever. Stryker carried forward Tugwell's agenda at the FSA: facilitate social change. Stryker's brief was to document the dire effects of the depression and dust bowl of the 1930s on the hundred of thousands of people who, starving and jobless, moved west in search of new lives, or who remained in distress on their tenant farms, almost reconciled to their fates. Even more, he was determined to demonstrate to the public through photographs the need for, and the accomplishments of, the New Deal programs in which he believed so deeply. He achieved this by careful research and planning—even scripting—of the photographic expeditions his staff undertook. He also hired the best. In addition to Lange, the FSA employed Arthur Rothstein, Walker Evans, Carl Mydans, Marion Post Wolcott, Ben Shahn, Jack Delano, John Vachon, Esther Bubley, and Russell Lee, among others.[39] In carrying forward the FSA photography, Stryker knew his goals and bent his cameramen to his ends.

The result is, for some, the most significant body of visual work created in the United States. Moreover, the FSA photography project had enormous long-term effects on photography, for it trained a generation of photographers and editors about the nature, purpose and methodology of documentary photography. Lange was a part, as well as a beneficiary, of both this photographic heritage and the methodology of Stryker.

When war finally came to the U.S. in 1941, the FSA was being whittled down. Some of its staff, such as Carl Mydans, became star photographers for magazines that covered the war;[40] others went to work for other government agencies such as the Office of War Information and, in the case of Lange, for the WRA.

Lange was hired to document all phases of the internment, from assembly centers to the camps themselves. While doing so, she apparently had sporadic trouble with the Army, which was in charge of the evacuation and transport of aliens and which barely recognized her as a government employee. Overall, she made 691 photographs for the WRA. In any event, the National Archives show that she made 235 photographs at Manzanar in two days, July 1 and July 2, 1942,[41] at a time when the camp was incomplete but functioning.

If Adams found Manzanar at its best, Lange undoubtedly saw it at its worst, or at a very low point indeed; evacuees were still being brought into it. When Albers had been there in April 1942, Manzanar was just being built by the Army and the American Japanese "pioneers." By the time Lange arrived the buildings were complete, but just barely. The single walls of the barracks had wide cracks through which the ever-present dust blew or, on a good day, just filtered. There were few interior partitions; the toilets and showers lacked any privacy, to the great distress of the modest and conservative American Japanese. The food was poor and often prepared by amateurs.[42] The library, schools and adult classes were just beginning; the *Manzanar Free Press* was edited by a Caucasian and printed by mimeograph. People were traumatized, confused and resentful. Family discipline was beginning to break down and there was little agreement among American Japanese as to how to respond to the outrage and insult that had been visited upon them. About five months after Lange's visit, the rising discontent and conflict among the evacuees exploded into a riot, the Army was called in, and the frightened, undisciplined, and poorly led troops opened fire and killed two innocent American Japanese.

Lange photographed the very beginnings of Manzanar becoming a self-sufficient town.[43] Evacuees had begun little vegetable gardens between the barracks; she showed them laboring in the hot sun. Children played the all-American game of baseball. Schools were just starting; attendance was voluntary and the classrooms primitive.

Lange's sense of outrage was fueled by the callousness exhibited by the military and the trampling of Americans' rights by their own government. She seemed to go out of her way to photographically note the indiscriminate hardships imposed on the evacuees by the Army that made no attempt to distinguish between the old, the infirm, and the hardy and able-bodied. Her revulsion showed in many but not in all of her images. In contrast to Adams, she photographed individuals, not as heroic figures, but as semi-tragic ones. People stand with tags in their coat lapels like so much luggage; children and adults alike look bewildered and resigned to an unknown fate. School children sit outdoors against tar-paper barracks walls; schools were neither built nor equipped. Two orphans sit in a bare room in the "Children's Village."

In a formal sense, also, when Lange photographed individuals, the result was strikingly different from Adams' portraits. She seldom framed the head alone; more likely, the whole figure and often some of its environment shows. She was interested in demonstrating the social context in which the subject existed; by contrast, Adams' portraits were meant, as we have said, to be heroic. They were classic portraits that expressed to Adams, if not to others, his theme that the inhabitants of Manzanar had overcome to a great extent the inevitable injustices of war; Lange's pictures were social statements that only obliquely condemned the internment. They do not convey the full measure of her outrage described by her friend and helper, Christina Gardner, who recalled one evening in May 1942, finding Lange in her hotel room, consumed by the horror of a day of photographing the exodus, "in some sort of paroxysm of fear" because of the erosion of civil liberties she was witnessing.[44]

Despite Lange's abhorrence of the relocation and the poignancy of many of her pictures, she did not create at the same high emotional level that she had enjoyed while working for Stryker. None of the Manzanar images quite reach the intensity that pervades her best work, such as the famous "Migrant Mother," although she made several touching images of the initial uprooting of the American Japanese from homes and businesses and their removal into the assembly centers. The saddest of these pictures shows aged Mr. Kondo sitting on an army cot in his tiny space at the Tanforan stables, erect but forlorn, with but a bare light bulb and a clock for decoration.[45] But her Manzanar work fails even to hint at the rising tension within the camp that ultimately led to violence.

How can we account for the difference between Lange's FSA work and her Manzanar pictures? For one thing, during the FSA period, Lange was guided by Stryker, and as much as she may have resented his control, in her very rebellion she permitted her innermost feelings to be engaged and expressed. But during her time with the WRA, she was married to Taylor, who had a cooler view of the relocation and may have influenced Lange, perhaps subconsciously.

Taylor, an agricultural economist, cited with approval General DeWitt's explanation of the military necessity for the relocation, and his contention that the American Japanese were a "national group, almost wholly unassimilated, which has preserved in large measure to itself, its customs and traditions, a group characterized by strong filial piety."[46]

Taylor complimented the Army, saying it had acted with "dispatch and courtesy."[47] He endorsed the report of the Tolan Committee of the House of Representatives, which argued that the relocation was indeed a military necessity. He expected that the "serious legal questions of constitutionality remain" but expected that they would be decided by the courts after "long and mature consideration…."[48]

Taylor's views about the internment seem at odds with those expressed by Lange, who was upset about what she thought were its gross violations of the civil rights of American Japanese. But it is speculative how much Taylor's perspective contributed to the dilution of pungency in Lange's Manzanar photographs.

Another aspect affected Lange's work. In the FSA tradition, she wanted social change and felt that her pictures contributed to it. But she had been trained by FSA's Stryker to make pictures to promote the New Deal programs. By becoming dependent on Stryker as one of his publicists, she necessarily stepped back from her own instincts in order to follow the dictates of her boss. Her well-known battles with Stryker were responses to Stryker's callous bureaucratic disregard for the documentarians' integrity. "Do you think I give a damn about a photographer's soul with Hitler at our doorstep? You are nothing but camera fodder to me," he proclaimed. [49] Paradoxically, even while struggling with Stryker, or perhaps because of it, Lange managed to look deeply into her subjects and produced great and searing photographs for the FSA. One wonders whether the stimulus of Stryker, or an editor like him, might have made her WRA work at Manzanar more compelling.

Finally, it is difficult to doubt that the official limitations and even harassment by the Army and the WRA affected her photographs; she was told where and when to work, and what not to record.

Camp chef by Dorothea Lange

Toyo Miyatake by Ansel Adams

TOYO MIYATAKE

Toyo Miyatake was born in Japan in 1895 and came to America when he was 14 years old. Originally, he wanted to become a painter, but about 1919 or 1920, he took up photography, and at the suggestion of a friend who recognized his talent, he began to study seriously with Los Angeles photographer Harry Shigeta. After five or six months, Shigeta shut down his classes and moved to Chicago, where he became a well-known illustration photographer. Miyatake also studied with Edward Weston during Weston's residence in the Los Angeles area, and soon he had a substantial reputation as a pictorial photographer.[50] He opened a photographic studio in Los Angeles' Little Tokyo district and continued his close friendship with Weston.[51]

When Miyatake went to Manzanar in 1942, he smuggled a lens into the camp; cameras were banned for internees and especially enemy aliens. He also constructed a makeshift camera and quietly photographed the camp. He was discovered after nine months and called into Merritt's office.[52] The Director told him that Edward Weston was concerned about him, and had written Merritt about him. [53]

Merritt permitted Miyatake to continue to photograph, at first accompanied by a Caucasian WRA employee who released the shutter. The first "helper" incurred Miyatake's wrath when he carelessly ruined an exposed film. He quit and was replaced by a series of wives of Caucasian employees, who went around with him or sat in the studio, and took the camera lens home at night. Later, the "accompanists" were abandoned after several people quit the pointless, boring job. Miyatake then worked on his own and recorded everyday life at Manzanar. Merritt allowed film to be mailed to Miyatake and permitted his professional equipment to be brought to the camp. A small darkroom and studio was established. All told, Miyatake made about 1500 exposures during his more than three years at the camp from 1942 to late 1945.[54]

The most extensive collection of Miyatake's work is found in *Toyo Miyatake Behind the Camera, 1923-1979*.[55] This book includes pre-war and post-war portraiture, sports and dance photographs, and pictures of Miyatake himself after the war, shown as the family patriarch and international luminary. About half of the book is comprised of Manzanar photographs; some duplicate those in the Manzanar High School Yearbook and a few have been published elsewhere.

Miyatake's Manzanar pictures frequently show the surrounding mountains, gray and looming ominously in the background. Unlike Adams' images in which the Sierras spring forward in pristine clarity, Miyatake's images speak of oppression and not of renewal.

Toyo Miyatake Behind the Camera, 1923-1979, like the Yearbook, documents a wide range of camp activities. Most of the pictures are straightforward, but a few show unusual scenes: an Army officer swearing in *Nisei* recruits; a group of American Japanese camp police; allegedly disloyal evacuees leaving for the Tule Lake camp where such people were segregated; a family leaving the camp; *Nisei* soldiers visiting friends and families; the dismantling of the camp buildings; and a sign on the Relocation Office marking the phasing out of Manzanar, from a cumulative total population of 11,061 to 2,891 on September 30, 1945, and 835 on November 8, 1945, two weeks before it was shut down.

Miyatake's Yearbook photographs are factual and objective; many seem casual, almost like snapshots. People go about their business, kids walk to school, sing in the choir, play baseball, study theater, woodworking, home economics, science, and farming. Some youngsters smile, but many do not. Classes are shown with their predominantly Caucasian teachers.[56] Groups look like they are in typical American schools, but in the background lurks the ugly barracks in which pupils slept and studied. Beyond that, there is a persistent bleak landscape, most unlike the grandeur Adams presented.

One picture shows three boys peering through a barbed wire fence. A guard tower with a searchlight on top shows in the upper right hand corner. Miyatake's son Archie thinks that the boys were inside looking out. The image is particularly touching because it violated the rule that camp guard towers and fences were never to be photographed.[57] At the end of the 1943-1944 High School Yearbook there is a picture of a guard tower, and two pages later, a hand with a wire cutter about to snip a strand of barbed wire, with a guard tower looming in the background. By 1944, it was too late and pointless to enforce the rule against such photographs; people had left Manzanar in large numbers; the nature of the "internment" was then generally known. Censorship, if it ever had a reason, was by then an anomaly.

When he was released from the camp a few weeks before it closed in November 1945, Miyatake returned to Los Angeles and reopened his studio. Archie had learned to photograph and retouch negatives at Manzanar and joined his father in the business. Toyo became a celebrity in both Los Angeles and in Japan. In 1993 the Los Angeles Community Redevelopment Agency commissioned Nobuho Nagasawa to sculpt an oversize bronze of his handmade camp camera. It is permanently displayed in Little Tokyo near the Japanese American National Museum.

Camp boundary marker by Toyo Miyatake

ELUSIVE TRUTH

The four Manzanar photographers worked at various times in a changing venue that was built, inhabited, depopulated, and swiftly dismantled in less than four years. They were each photographing different scenes and for disparate reasons. Moreover, the social climate within Manzanar underwent constant shifts from hostility and friction to acceptance to near-nostalgia by a few. The target was moving before their cameras.

Lange was usually blunt, yet her Manzanar work lacks the full measure of the pathos she mustered while working for FSA. Notwithstanding her strongly expressed feelings about the relocation program, we find little in the WRA pictures close to the emotional intensity of "Migrant Mother," "Migratory Cotton Picker," "Woman of the High Plains," or "Fifty-Seven Year Old Sharecropper Woman, Mississippi."

On the other hand, while we know nothing from verbal or written sources about Albers' response to the American Japanese plight, his photographs skewer the evacuation program when he shows confused elderly victims and bemused children, an ironic contrast to the government's concerns about subversion and military crisis.

Adams, as has been demonstrated, tried to see a positive side to the experience, an effort that outraged his friend Lange. However, he was not oblivious to the hardships imposed on innocent people; working much later than Lange, he felt that they had overcome for the most part the effects of injustice.

Miyatake had a longer time to record Manzanar—he and his family were there from almost the beginning until the very end of the camp—yet he photographed at the sufferance of the camp administration and could not express all of his feelings with impunity. Looking closely at his published work, we perceive, as he must have, the tension between people who have been abused and their need to simply live as comfortably and productively as possible. If his images are often prosaic, it must be kept in mind that he saw his task to be that of documenting the everyday life of Manzanar. Even in doing that, he must have had to tread lightly to avoid the fractious disputes among the internees.

Unknown to all four photographers, however, was the secret that the material with which they worked was generated by a lie initiated by the government. No one can say how their Manzanar work would have been affected had they discovered the truth, or if they would have undertaken it at all.

Of the four photographers, only Adams wrote extensively about his views of the evacuation of the American Japanese. The captions written by Lange for her Manzanar pictures are simple and convey little of her sense of outrage. What Albers' reaction to the relocation was we can only infer from his photographs, and to some extent, from the extensive captions he wrote for them that carried forward his ironic thrust. Like Lange and Albers, Miyatake apparently did not write an explanation of his pictures or about his reactions to his incarceration and that of his family.

At Manzanar, each of the four photographers established a distinctive theme, and each told an aspect of the truth. None of them, however, integrated their work into the format of a picture story such as those produced by W. Eugene Smith or Henri Cartier-Bresson. One might speculate—although I hesitate to do so—what the results would have been if a strong editorial mind like that of Stryker had guided their projects.

Moreover, each of the Manzanar photographers worked under external constraints that shaped and limited their photography. There was an understandable reluctance and even fear to challenge the government in time of war. Miyatake was in effect a prisoner and his right to photograph in the camp was tenuous. Lange and Albers worked directly for the WRA and were therefore subject to its rules and policies. Adams' viewpoint was his own, although it was heavily influenced by his friendship with Merritt and perhaps by an inability to empathize with, and understand, a dispossessed minority who had lost so much, not only in liberty and property, but also in cultural coherence. All of these elements should be weighed in considering the Manzanar photographs.

It may be that, unlike a witness's oath to tell the "whole truth," the documentary photograph is inherently limited in what it can show and how deeply it can cut.

But that constraint is not inflexible. As the history of this genre demonstrates, knowledge, skill and even daring can peel back layers of opaque rind and reveal a reality that would be missed at first glance. If some of the Manzanar photographs individually seem at a casual glance to be bland expressions of a significant moment in American history, their cumulative effect is substantial and moving.

Taken together, the ordinary scenes of the daily life made by Miyatake, the poignant images of Lange, the proud portraits of Adams, and the ironic photographs of Albers, indelibly record a stain on America's professed belief in the worth and dignity of each individual. Though the whole truth was elusive, the four photographers together captured enough of it to show Manzanar as both a failure of American freedom and a triumph of human spirit.

Notes

[1] The first Director of the WRA was Milton Eisenhower, brother of the general and later President. He became distressed at the abridgement of citizens' rights and quit after three months. He was succeeded by Dillon S. Myer, a seasoned bureaucrat whose expertise was agriculture. For Myer's perspective, see Myer, *Uprooted Americans*.

[2] See: Marc Reisner, *Cadillac Desert: The American West and Its Disappearing Water*.

[3] Ralph Merritt, a Sierra Club friend of Ansel Adams, took over as Director of Manzanar in late 1943. He had some experience with Japanese people because he worked for a time in Japan as a representative of Sun-Maid Raisins. Merritt was well-liked by many American Japanese; while in camp, Toyo Miyatake made an oil painting of him that he presented to Merritt, who appreciated it very much.

[4] In Ex parte Endo.

[5] See Ilen H. Eaton, *Beauty Behind Barbed Wire; The Arts of the Japanese in Our War Relocation Camps*. This book contains some photographs by Toyo Miyatake and Clem Albers. For a description of life in the Manzanar camp, see Houston, *Farewell to Manzanar*.

[6] The pay ranged from $12 for unskilled labor to $19 per month for highly skilled professionals such as doctors and nurses. One reason for the low pay was the sensitivity of the WRA to criticism from right wing and racist groups who claimed it was "coddling" the evacuees.

[7] As early as the fall of 1942, Assistant Secretary of War John McCloy urged a loyalty review of the evacuees as the first step in forming a *Nisei* combat unit. Colonel Bendetsen, the Army lawyer who had organized the exclusion scheme, began to waver, admitting that maybe his ideas about the inscrutability of the Japanese were "cock-eyed." However, he opposed a loyalty review program because it would confess to "an original mistake of terrifically horrible proportions." John Hersey essay in John Armor and Peter Wright, ed. *Manzanar*, p. 57-58.

[8] TenBroeck, Barnhart and Matson, *Prejudice, War and the Constitution*, p. 170-174.

[9] In 1986, when Gordon Hirabayashi sought to vacate his wartime conviction for violating the curfew and exclusion orders, the Ninth Circuit Court of Appeals ruled for him because the government had unjustly suppressed evidence by withholding DeWitt's original report that was "based upon racial prejudice rather than military exigency." The Court agreed with Hirabayashi that had the Supreme Court known the truth, its decision would probably have been different. Writing for the Court, Appeals Judge Schroeder stated:

"The Hirabayashi and Korematsu decisions have never occupied an honored place in our history. …. [Research materials] demonstrate that there could have been no reasonable military assessment of an emergency at the time, that the orders were based upon racial stereotypes, and that the orders caused needless suffering and shame for thousands of American citizens….

The event which triggered the lawsuit occurred in 1982, when an archival researcher discovered the sole remaining copy of the original report prepared by the general who issued the curfew and exclusion orders. War Department officials revised the report in several material respects and tried to destroy the original report at the time its attorneys were preparing briefs in the Hirabayashi and Korematsu cases. ….

This record contains a memo by Theodore Smith of the Civil Affairs Division of the Western Defense Command dated June 29, 1943, certifying that he witnessed the burning of 'the gallery proofs, galley pages, drafts and memorandums of the original report of the Japanese Evacuation.' ….

The district court further found that the United States government doctored the documentary record to reflect that DeWitt had made a judgment of military exigency ….[and] that had the suppressed material been submitted to the Supreme Court, its decision probably would have been materially affected.

The government also agrees with the petitioner and the district court that General DeWitt acted on the basis of his own racist views and not on the basis of any military judgment that time was of the essence". <u>Hirabayashi v. United States</u>, 828 F2d 591 (9th Cir., 1987).

[10] The Photographic Division consisted of an Information Specialist, an Assistant I.S., a Head Photographer, and two clerks.

[11] For example, many of Lange's WRA photographs bear an "impounded" mark on a margin, although the stamp does not show on any of the National Archives scans.

There is also an extensive WRA archive at the University of California at http://www.oac.cdlib.org/dynaweb/ead/calher/jvac. It contains about 7000 prints and 317 Kodachrome slides. Lange made 691 of the photographs of which 209 (235 according to the National Archives) were done at Manzanar.

[12] The WRA and the Army (which administered the first phase of the program, the assembly and initial screening of people, and their transfer to relocation camps), wanted a photographic record of these events, but not necessarily a public record. Over 25,000 photographs of the exclusion and relocation activity were made; only few made it into General DeWitt's report to the War Department, and they were selected to show how happy the evacuees were with their "considerate" treatment by their government. Judith

Fryer Davidov, "'The Color of My Skin, the Shape of My Eyes': Photographs of the American Japanese Internment by Dorothea Lange, Ansel and Adams, and Toyo Miyatake," *Yale Journal of Criticism*, vol. 9 No. 2, p. 223-244; Ohrn, *Dorothea Lange and the Documentary Tradition*, p. 146-148.

Clearly, the Relocation Centers were not extermination camps; there was some brutality by guards and even loss of life at the camps, but most reports indicate that it was occasional and against policy. Two American Japanese were killed at Manzanar by the military police during a riot that involved hostility towards inmates who were accused of siding with the authorities and informing for them. To equate the relocation program with the Nazi camps in which millions of people were murdered would be obscene. Yet, that does not excuse the wrong done to American Japanese.

[13] It is interesting to speculate as to the criteria the censors used in passing upon potential photographic subject matter and in actually suppressing photographs. Given the government's line that it was militarily necessary to move American Japanese away from the West Coast where they might help an invasion or an aerial attack, or sabotage the naval and military bases and aircraft plants, and that the American Japanese were compliant and accepting of their ill fate, even to the point of imprisonment in the camps, why were pictures of the barbed wire enclosures, the guard towers with machine guns and searchlights forbidden?

[14] He was born in 1902.

[15] Some of Adams well-known distaste for Steichen may have come from this encounter. In the author's conversations with Adams, it was clear that there were aesthetic and philosophical differences as well. See also, Alinder & Stillman, infra, n.16, p.145.

[16] There are several excellent sources about Adams and his work. For example: Mary Alinder, *Ansel Adams, A Biography*; Jonathan Spaulding, *Ansel Adams and the American Landscape; Ansel Adams—Letters and Images, 1916-1984*, ed. by Mary Street Alinder and Andrea Gray Stillman; *Ansel Adams—An Autobiography* (with Mary Street Alinder).

[17] Alinder & Stillman, supra n.16, p.184 (letter to Nancy Newhall, 1943).

[18] ibid., p. 145.

[19] "Born Free and Equal" was shown at the Museum of Modern Art after considerable debate among the Trustees and after the name of the show was changed from "Born Free and Equal" to simply "Manzanar," and the text of the Fourteenth Amendment and a statement by Abraham Lincoln were removed. It was hung in a basement gallery at MOMA. Many copies of the book were burned by self-proclaimed patriots, and it is rumored, but never documented, by the publisher itself. Thus the book is now quite rare and sells in good condition for as much as $500.

[20] To date, they are catalogued but only a handful have been digitized.

[21] supra n.7. See also reproductions in Jerry Stanley, *I Am An American*.

[22] View cameras are useful for landscapes because they have controls that allow for correction of unwanted distortions and permit enhanced depth of field; the Zeiss camera was much like a view camera, but more compact and easily used, especially indoors. Both types are used on a tripod and require focusing on a ground glass with a dark cloth over the photographer's head and camera back to keep out the light so the image can be seen. These larger format cameras were slow to operate, but they generated more delicate and precise detail than was possible with miniature films in the 1940s. With the Graflex, the image appears via a mirror onto the ground glass that is seen at the end of a vertical leather hood. When the exposure is made, the mirror flips up, allowing the light to travel to the back of the camera where the film is exposed. Such a camera is well-suited for portraits because a subjects' expressions and the picture's composition can be monitored until the moment of exposure. Moreover, unlike view cameras, the Graflex can be hand-held, adding to its flexibility.

[23] Adams was very unhappy with the reproduction quality

of the prints in *Born Free and Equal*. He chalked it up to the wartime lack of good paper.

[24] *Ansel Adams—An Autobiography*, supra n.16, p. 260.

[25] Photographic portraits are notoriously ambiguous in trying to reflect the inner feelings of subjects. Photographers and viewers read into such pictures the results that they assume. Thus some of Adams' "heroic" heads may really have reflected only stoical acceptance of injustice.

[26] The smiles should not be taken at face value. First, Adams was a warm, ebullient figure with an expressive and engaging manner. I always felt that he could coax a smile from a boulder! Second, to the camp inmates he was a stranger, and smiles are often used to allay hostility and avoid confrontation.

[27] *Dorothea Lange and the Documentary Tradition*, supra n.12, p. 124.

[28] There is no evidence that Adams possessed any extensive knowledge of Japanese tradition and culture. Adams' primary contact with Japanese, other than with Miyatake as a fellow professional, was with Harry Oye, a servant of the family. Adams met Miyatake during his visits to Manzanar.

[29] It occurred on December 6, 1942.

[30] supra n. 4, 1944.

[31] *Ansel Adams—An Autobiography*, supra n.16, p. 260.

[32] Many thought that WRA's process of determining loyalty was grossly unfair. Those who resisted the WRA were branded as disloyal to the U.S. and segregated in lockups at Tule Lake.

[33] *Born Free and Equal*, supra n. 19, p. 102.

[34] Richard Drinnon, *Keeper of Concentration Camps: Dillon S, Myer and American Racism*, pp. 43-49. Both Merritt and WRA Director Dillon S. Myer shared a patronizing view of the American Japanese inmates. Merritt once referred to Manzanar residents as "my children;" Myer had no faith in the American Japanese's ability to govern their own communities or make decisions for themselves. He wanted to be the boss. Ibid. p. 7-8.

[35] Interview conducted by the Regional Oral History Office of the Bancroft Library, University of California at Berkeley, located at http://www.book.uci.edu/BornFree/bornfreeinter-1.html.

[36] Albers' photographs appear to be made with a 4x5 camera, the size used by most press photographers of the time. The most popular of these cameras was the Speed Graphic that was equipped with a rangefinder, viewfinder, and sometimes, a rapid film changer magazine.

Joe Rosenthal, Albers' close friend, graciously provided much information about Albers' personality and professional skills in a telephone interview January 1, 1999. According to Rosenthal, Albers was self-effacing, highly insightful, and understood dimensions of a story that others might overlook. He had great rapport with the subjects he worked with, and being an avid reader, he brought a depth of understanding as well as experience to his work.

[37] Maisie and Richard Conrat, *Executive Order 9066*. Ten images by Miyatake were included in Stanley, *I Am An American*, supra n. 21.

[38] Karen Becker Ohrn's *Dorothea Lange and the Documentary Tradition* is a recommended biography of this influential photographer.

[39] Roy Emerson Stryker and Nancy Wood, *In This Proud Land*.

[40] Mydans joined *Life* magazine after he was released from a long captivity by the Japanese and repatriated. He photographed a *Life* picture story on the allegedly disloyal American Japanese held in a stockade at Tule Lake. March 20, 1944.

[41] There is no book devoted exclusively to Lange's Manzanar work. Some appear in Conrat, *Executive Order 9066*, supra n. 37; Ohrn, *Dorothea Lange*, supra n.12; and Davidov, *The Color of My Skin*, supra n.12.

[42] *Farewell to Manzanar*, supra n. 5.

[43] Years later, an evacuee recalled meeting in 1966 a Caucasian woman photographer (undoubtedly Lange) who had worked at Manzanar. "I could scarcely speak to her," she said. It was not the bad memories. Rather it was "simply

her validation that all those things had taken place." Jeanne Houston, *Farewell to Manzanar*, supra n. 5, p. 187 (Bantam ed.).

[44] *Dorothea Lange—A Visual Life*, ed. by Elizabeth Partridge, Ch. 4, Essay by Roger Daniels, p. 50.

[45] *Executive Order 9066*, supra n. 37, p. 94.

[46] Paul S. Taylor, "Our Stakes in the Japanese Exodus," 31 *Survey Graphic*, No. 9, September 1942, page 373 ff.

[47] Ibid., p. 375.

[48] Ibid., p. 375

[49] Letter to Jack Delano, quoted in Jonathan Green, *A Critical History of American Photography*, p. 42.

[50] It is not clear exactly when Miyatake and Weston first met. Weston lived in the Los Angeles area from 1909 to 1923, and after his return from Mexico, from 1926 to 1929. Ten of Miyatake's prints were included in the show "California Pictorialism." The catalog was published by the San Francisco Museum of Modern Art in 1977. The photographs were made between 1923 and 1937.

[51] Much valuable information about Miyatake's pre-war life and his activities at Manzanar was graciously provided by his son, Archie, during a telephone interview on December 29, 1998.

Toyo Miyatake is, unfortunately, little known outside of photography circles. Many of his photographs have been reproduced without attribution. In addition to the republished Manzanar High School Year Book (infra n. 54), his pictures appear in *Two Views of Manzanar*, 1978, a catalog of a show of his work and that of Ansel Adams at the Wight Gallery at UCLA, infra, n. 52. See also *Toyo Miyatake Behind the Camera 1923-1979*, ed. by Atsufumi Miyatake, Taisuke Fujishima, and Eiko Hosoe. (Text in Japanese.) Four photographs also appear in Patrick Nagatani, "Virtual Pilgrimage," essay by Jasmine Alinder.

[52] G. Howe, P. Nagatani, S. Rankin, *Two Views of Manzanar*, p. 10.

[53] *Toyo Miyatake: Documenting Japanese Internment*, Knowledge Adventure, 1998, http://www.letsfindout.com/subjects/ america/toyo.html; Hosoe section "Toyo and Edward" in *Toyo Miyatake Behind the Camera 1923-1979*, supra n. 51, p. 144-145.

[54] Some of Miyatake's work at Manzanar has recently been re-published in *Our World—1943-44, the Manzanar High School Yearbook* through the efforts of Diane Yotsuya Honda. This edition also contains interesting biographical information about Miyatake. The last page shows a hand holding a wire cutter poised to clip a strand of barbed wire. Houston, supra n. 5, writes that this image was taken for and published in the following year's Yearbook. Miyatake's son Archie was a member of the Manzanar High class of 1944. He has retired from the Toyo Miyatake Studio in San Gabriel, California. He was given a grant by the Civil Liberties Public Education Fund to restore his father's Manzanar negatives and scan them onto the World Wide Web. The scans are now at the Japanese American National Museum and should soon become available on the Web.

[55] supra n. 51.

[56] One photograph in the Yearbook shows Ansel Adams, (unidentified, and without his trademark beard) photographing a drama class.

[57] Jasmine Alinder, "Toyo Miyatake's 'Boys Behind Barbed Wire,'" *Journal of the International Institute*, University of Michigan, vol. 6, no. 1, Fall, 1998. Alinder shows how this compelling Miyatake photograph was published without attribution and used to illustrate an article out of context, and indeed, in violation of the intended meaning of the image.

Probably by the time Miyatake made this particular photograph, the rules against leaving the enclosure had been greatly relaxed. As the alleged "military threat" became even foggier than the high Sierra passes in winter, inmates were allowed to work, hike, and camp at considerable distances from Manzanar. Those preparing to leave were permitted to visit Lone Pine and other nearby towns, and the locals visited Manzanar to play baseball and other sports.

A son visiting his parents before shipping out by Toyo Miyatake

PORTFOLIO

Manzanar Free Press

Ansel Adams

Manzanar Free Press

Electrician

Miyatake family

Manzanar street

Shohara

Choir

Spanish–American War Veteran

Manzanar photography show

Family leaving camp

Clouds over the Sierras

Working the fields

Electrician

Miyatake family

Manzanar street

Shohara

Choir

Spanish−American War Veteran

Manzanar photography show

Family leaving camp

Clouds over the Sierras

Working the fields

Children being trucked

Clem Albers

Children being trucked

Manzanar military polcie

Child on the way to Manzanar

Blind man arriving at Manzanar

Dr. Goto treating an elderly patient in the camp hospital

Getting water from community source

Mealtime

Geta—sandals good for dusty streets

Girl wearing geta

Manzanar military police

Child on the way to Manzanar

Blind man arriving at Manzanar

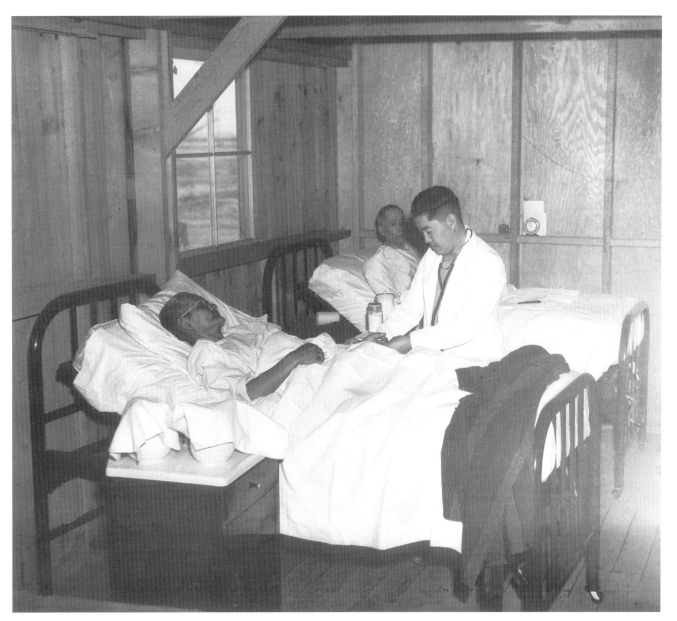

Dr. Goto treating an elderly patient in the camp hospital

Getting water from community source

Mealtime

Geta—samdals good for dusty streets

Girl wearing geta

Guyuale lathe house

Dorothea Lange

Guyuale lathe house

Flag and dust storm

Manzanar winter street

Young internee

Joe Blamey (born in Japan)

Children studying, outside school

Family quarters

Internee gardener

Nurse with orphaned babies

Flag and dust storm

Manzanar winter street

Young internee

Joe Blamey (born in Japan)

Children studying, outside school

Family quarters

Internee gardener

Nurse with orphaned babies

Toyo Miyatake's darkroom (Hisao Kimura, George Shiba and Archie Miyatake)

Toyo Miyatake

Toyo Miyatake's darkroom

Remains of first aid station after completion of barracks

Japanese garden after snowstorm

Dust storm

Dance lessons at grammar school

Manzanar mounted police led by Joe Saiki

Picnic at Bairs Creek

Mr. Ishida, cultivating chrysanthemums

Pounding rice to make *mochi*

Owens Valley fruit orchard

Cloud forms over Manzanar

Toy center

Laboratory technician at Manzanar Hospital

Apple blossoms, Mount Williamson

Watchtower

Shiba family visiting Hashimoto family and new baby

Grieving mother

Remains of first aid station after completion of barracks

Japanese garden after snowstorm

Dust storm

Dance lessons at grammar school

Manzanar mounted police led by Joe Saiki (second from right)

Picnic at Bairs Creek (Shigeji Kuwahara, Kazuko Yamazaki, George Shiba and Mona Kinoshita)

Mr. Ishida, cultivating chrysanthemums

Pounding rice to make mochi *(rice cake), a Japanese New Year's tradition*

Owens Valley fruit orchard

Cloud forms over Manzanar

Toy center (toys donated by Quakers; due to baggage limitations, very few toys were brought by internees)

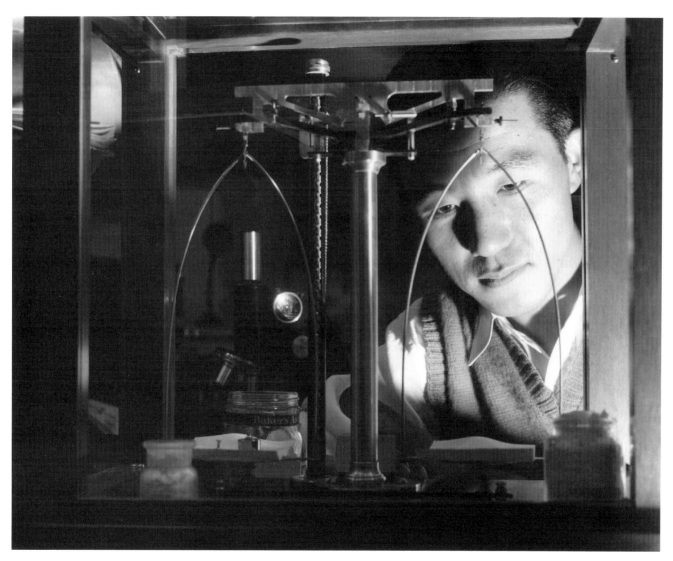

Laboratory technician at Manzanar Hospital

Apple blossoms, Mount Williamson

Watchtower

Shiba family visiting Hashimoto family and new baby

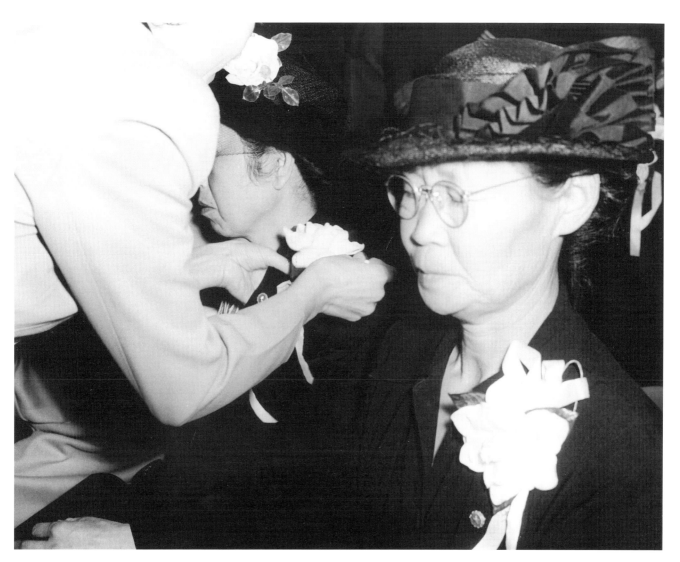

Grieving mother of PFC Frank Arikawa, killed in combat

BIBLIOGRAPHY

Alinder, Jasmine. "Toyo Miyatake's 'Boys Behind Barbed Wire,'" *Journal of the International Institute*, University of Michigan, vol. 6, no. 1, Fall, 1998.

Alinder, Mary Street and Stillman, Andrea Gray, ed. *Ansel Adams—Letters and Images, 1916-1984*, New York Graphic Society, Little, Brown and Company, 1988.

Alinder, Mary. *Ansel Adams, A Biography*, Henry Holt and Company, 1996.

Ansel Adams—An Autobiography (with Mary Street Alinder), New York Graphic Society, Little Brown and Company, 1985.

Armor, John and Wright, Peter, ed., *Manzanar*, Vintage, 1989.

Born Free and Equal, U.S. Camera, 1944.

California Pictorialism. Exhibit catalog, San Francisco Museum of Modern Art. 1977.

Conrat, Maisie and Richard. *Executive Order 9066*, California Historical Society, 1972

Davidov, Judith Fryer. "'The Color of My Skin, the Shape of My Eyes': Photographs of the American Japanese Internment by Dorothea Lange, Ansel and Adams, and Toyo Miyatake," *Yale Journal of Criticism*, vol. 9 No. 2.

Drinnon, Richard. *Keeper of Concentration Camps: Dillon S, Myer and American Racism*, University of California Press, 1987.

Eaton, Ilen H. *Beauty Behind Barbed Wire; The Arts of the Japanese in Our War Relocation Camps*, Harper & Brothers, 1952.

Ex parte Endo, 323 U.S. 283 (1944).

Green, Jonathan. *A Critical History of American Photography*, Harry N. Abrams, Inc., 1984.

Hirabayashi v. United States, 828 F2d 591 (9th Cir., 1987).

Houston, Jeanne W. and James D. *Farewell to Manzanar*, Bantam, 1995.

Howe, G., Nagatani, P., and Rankin, S. *Two Views of Manzanar*. Exhibit catalog, Frederick S. Wight Art Gallery, UCLA, 1978.

Miyatake, Atsufumi , Fujishima, Taisuke and Hosoe, Eiko, ed. *Toyo Miyatake Behind the Camera 1923-1979*, Tokyo, Bungeishunju, 1984.

Myer, Dillon S. *Uprooted Americans*, University of Arizona Press, 1971.

Nagatani, Patrick. "Virtual Pilgrimage," essay by Jasmine Alinder, Albuquerque Museum, 1998.

National Archives website (http://www.archives.gov)

Ohrn, Karen Becker. *Dorothea Lange and the Documentary Tradition*, Louisiana State University Press, 1980.

Our World—1943-44, the Manzanar High School Yearbook.

Partridge, Elizabeth, ed. *Dorothea Lange—A Visual Life.*

Reisner, Marc. *Cadillac Desert: The American West and Its Disappearing Water*, rev. ed., Penguin, 1993.

Spaulding, Jonathan. *Ansel Adams and the American Landscape*, Univ. of California Press, 1995.

Stanley, Jerry. *I Am An American*, Crown, 1994

Stryker, Roy Emerson and Wood, Nancy. *In This Proud Land*, Galahad Books, 1973.

Taylor, Paul S. "Our Stakes in the Japanese Exodus," 31 *Survey Graphic*, No. 9, September 1942.

TenBroeck, Barnhart and Matson, *Prejudice, War and the Constitution*, University of California Press, 1968.

War Relocation Authority Photographs of Japanese-American Evacuation and Resettlement, Bancroft Library, University of California, Berkeley, California. (http://www.oac.cdblib.org/dynaweb/ead/calher/jvac/.)

LIST OF ILLUSTRATIONS

INDEX

Publisher's Note

One of the great pleasures of publishing is meeting gentlemen like Archie Miyatake, whose father is one of the photographers featured in this book. Archie was interned at Manzanar as a young boy with his family, and he graduated from high school there. He returned with his family to Los Angeles when the camp was decommissioned. The Miyatakes reopened their photography studio, which operates to this day under the care of Archie and the third generation of Miyatakes. I want to thank Archie for sharing his time with me. His kindness and generosity are deeply appreciated.

Carl Mautz, July, 2002